Take Action

Parent Handout Workbook

Contents

Who can use Take Action?

The evidence-base for Take Action has been established with the program being delivered by registered psychologists, clinical psychologists, school psychologists and school guidance counsellors who are trained and experienced in Cognitive-Behavioural Therapy (CBT). Therefore, Take Action is recommended for use by these mental health and educational professionals. This Parent Handout Workbook should only be used in conjunction with the Take Action Practitioner Guidebook.

www.
AUSTRALIANACADEMIC**PRESS**
.com.au

Other titles in the Take Action program:
Take Action Child Handout Workbook
Take Action Practitioner Guidebook

Take Action Parent Handout Workbook
First published 2016
Australian Academic Press Group Pty. Ltd.
18 Victor Russell Drive
Samford Valley QLD 4520
Australia
www.australianacademicpress.com.au

Text copyright © 2016 Allison Waters and Trisha Groth

Illustrations copyright © 2016 Australian Academic Press Group Pty. Ltd

ISBN 9781922117298

Cover and text design by Maria Biaggini of The Letter Tree.

Cartoons and illustrations by Karen Mounsey-Smith of Gidgeymo Illustrations.

A Be AWARE

WELCOME to the Take Action program

The first step in the ACTION plan teaches children to be AWARE of their feelings and recognise when they feel anxious. Children will also learn to be AWARE of signals in their bodies that indicate they are feeling anxious.

Parenting can be a rewarding **and** challenging experience.

When a child experiences anxiety to the point where they miss out on enjoying some things in life, parents are presented with many challenges.

Often parents want to help their child but are not sure what to do, or they have already tried numerous things in the past.

The Take Action program has been designed to assist children and their families in managing anxiety.

Children (and their parents) will learn how to cope with and manage anxiety by Taking

ACTION

Taking ACTION against anxiety can help children enjoy life and be happy!

Children will create a Strong Team — a supportive network of people that can help them to take ACTION against their anxiety. It would be great if parents can start being part of their child's Strong Team straight away. This means that you will help your child practise the new skills they will learn, and provide support and encouragement to them as they progress through the Take Action program.

It is important to check with your child and see what they are learning and what Home Tasks they have to complete each week. The skills learnt in the Take Action program need to become a part of your child's daily life if they are to reduce their anxiety.

Take Action

Structure of the Take Action program

Parents are a very important part of the Take Action program. Parents will be introduced to the principles of the program, in addition to learning helpful parenting strategies that will assist them in encouraging their child to take ACTION against anxiety.

Step in the ACTION Plan	Child Content	Parent Content
	Introduction to the Take Action program	Introduction to the Take Action program
A Be AWARE	Learning to recognise signs of anxiety	Instruction about the Be AWARE and Keep CALM steps
C Keep CALM	Learning relaxation techniques	—
T THINK Strong Thoughts	Learning to THINK positive, ACTION-oriented thoughts	Instruction about the THINK Strong Thoughts step
I Get INTO Action	Learning to approach anxiety-provoking situations	Instruction about the Get INTO Action step
O Use my OPTIONS	Learning additional coping strategies	Instruction about the Use my OPTIONS and NEVER stop taking ACTION steps
N NEVER stop taking ACTION	Learning to use all the steps in the ACTION plan to keep taking ACTION against anxiety	Instruction about the NEVER stop taking ACTION steps
Booster	Review of the program	Review of the program

What is anxiety in children?

Anxiety is a common emotion that we all experience. Everyone feels scared or worried at some time — it is a normal part of life.

Anxiety is a signal that there is danger. In the caveman days, it was very important for cavemen to get scared if they saw a sabre-tooth tiger so they could either fight the tiger or run away to safety (see below).

That's a tiger.
He could eat me!
Should I run or fight?

Real DANGER!

It is normal to feel scared when you are in real danger, but sometimes children get scared or worried when they don't need to. Things like making new friends or being in the dark or being away from their parents might seem extremely scary to some children. These "false alarms" are not really dangerous but children might THINK they are. Children can learn that making new friends can be lots of fun and that they can be safe even when it is dark or when they are on their own.

All children experience anxiety as part of normal development. Many fears such as fear of the dark, fear of being away from parents and fear of strangers are normal and common aspects of child development and are thought to help protect children from danger and harm. However, when children experience excessive distress or they find it difficult to do things that other children of their age are capable of doing (because of their worries or fears), anxiety can be considered a problem.

Anxiety is one of the most common problems in children.
Estimates differ, but approximately 1 in 10 children
experience high levels of anxiety.

Types of anxiety in children

Children (and adults) experience anxiety in different ways. The Take Action program has been designed to target four different types of anxiety in children:

Generalised Anxiety: Children who have a general tendency to be worried about a range of life areas. Children typically worry about future events, past behaviour, academic or athletic achievement, friends, and health. Children often engage in excessive reassurance seeking, are often perfectionistic and highly conscientious. A number of physical complaints are usually reported including sleep disturbance, feeling tired, general feelings of tension (e.g., easily annoyed or grumpy) and an inability to relax.

Separation Anxiety: Children who fear being separated from a main caregiver, usually their mother or father. Children become extremely distressed and frightened whenever they become separated from their caregiver, and may try to avoid things like school or sleeping alone. Children with separation anxiety also worry about the possibility of being kidnapped, and accidents or death occurring, either to themselves or their caregiver. Children often report a number of physical complaints such as headaches, stomach aches or general sickness, especially upon impending separation.

Social Anxiety: Children who fear and/or avoid social situations where they have to interact with other people or be the centre of attention. Children often think others will evaluate them negatively or that they will embarrass themselves.

Specific Fears: Children who have excessive fear of a specific object, activity or situation and avoid this object, activity or situation. Some of the common types of specific phobias in children are fears of animals, natural environment (e.g., darkness, storms, water), blood and / or injections, and situations like elevators.

 Take Action | Parent Handout Workbook |

What causes anxiety in children?

There is no one factor that causes anxiety in children. Anxiety is due to a mix of factors which is likely to be different for every child. Some of these factors include:

Traumatic Event

A child who experiences a traumatic event (e.g., is severely bullied at school) may develop intense fear of this event (e.g., school and / or bullies).

Child Factors

- Temperament of the child — children can be born with an anxious temperament (e.g., shy, reactive, emotional vs. laid back).

- Biology / Genetics — anxiety seems to run in families. Children may have a highly-reactive nervous system (e.g., they are sensitive and quick to react to potential signs of danger).

- Way the child thinks — more likely to 'see' danger in the situation and underestimate his/her ability to cope in the situation (e.g., "What if....").

Learning Factors

Children are influenced by their environment, family, parents, school and peers

- Observation (e.g., seeing a parent frightened by a dog).

- Information they receive (e.g., if a child falls over and a parent shows they are extremely distressed by this, the child may learn that falling over is a terrible thing that should be avoided at all costs).

- Accidental rewards (e.g., a hug is given when they are anxious).

- Avoidance of anxiety-provoking situation — this maintains the child's anxiety about the situation / object.

Activity

Think about the factors that might be important for your child's anxiety.

Place an X in the box next to each relevant factor and think about why this factor may be important for your child.

☐ Traumatic events (describe)

_____

☐ Temperament (describe)

_____

☐ Biology / Genetics (describe)

_____

☐ Way your child thinks (describe)

_____

☐ Observation (describe)

_____

☐ Information your child receives (describe)

_____

☐ Accidental rewards (describe)

_____

☐ Avoidance (describe)

_____

Cycle of Anxiety in children

The figure below shows the three response systems of anxiety in children.

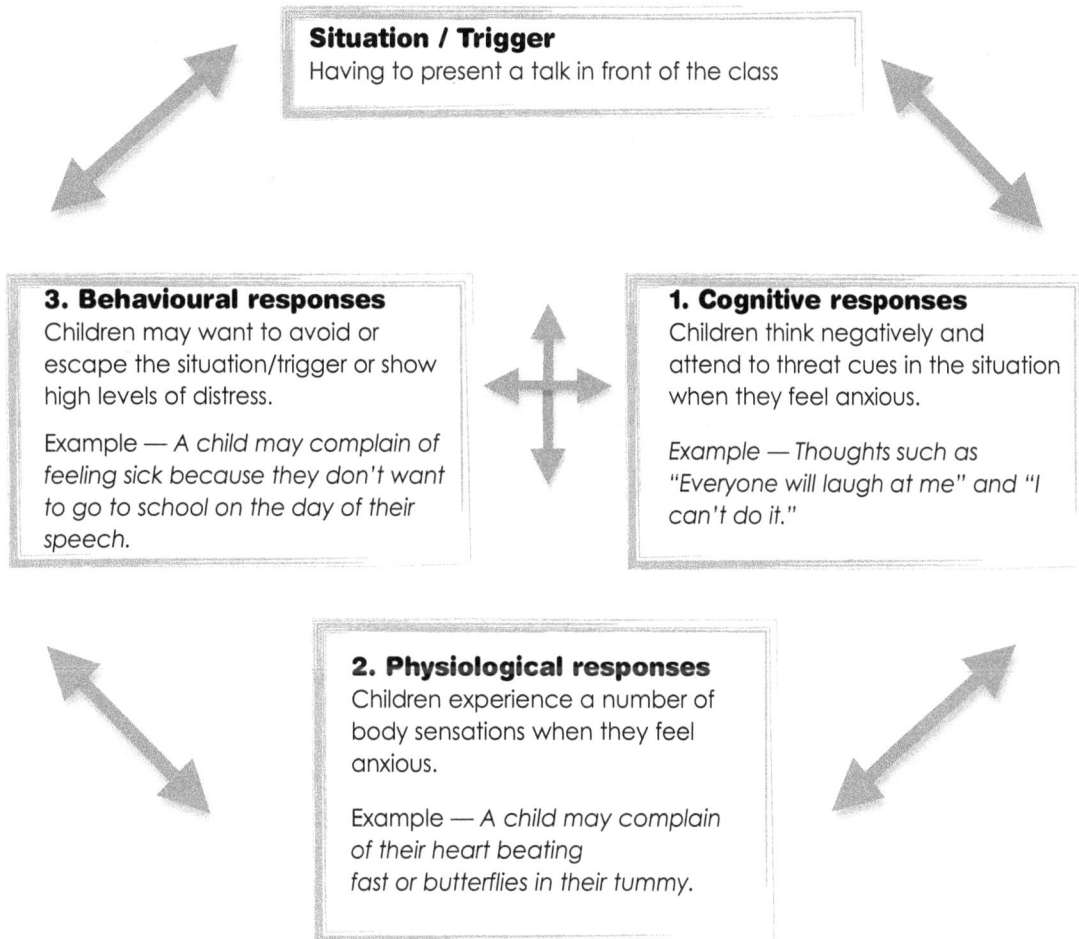

Situation / Trigger
Having to present a talk in front of the class

3. Behavioural responses
Children may want to avoid or escape the situation/trigger or show high levels of distress.

Example — *A child may complain of feeling sick because they don't want to go to school on the day of their speech.*

1. Cognitive responses
Children think negatively and attend to threat cues in the situation when they feel anxious.

Example — *Thoughts such as "Everyone will laugh at me" and "I can't do it."*

2. Physiological responses
Children experience a number of body sensations when they feel anxious.

Example — *A child may complain of their heart beating fast or butterflies in their tummy.*

How can the Take Action program assist children and families?

The Take Action program aims to teach children helpful ways to cope with and manage anxiety by addressing the Three Responses of Anxiety. The word ACTION is a coping-oriented acronym used throughout the program. Children are encouraged to *Take ACTION* against their anxiety (e.g., approach their fears/worries) using the well-researched and effective strategies learnt during the program.

Children will learn about an ACTION plan, with each letter in the word ACTION standing for a set of skills that children will learn during the program (described below):

Steps in the ACTION Plan

Be AWARE — The first step in the ACTION plan teaches children to be AWARE of their feelings and learn to recognise when they feel anxious. Children will also learn to be AWARE of signals in their bodies that indicate they are feeling anxious.

Keep CALM — Once children learn to be AWARE of signs of anxiety, the second step in the ACTION plan teaches children strategies to keep CALM and reduce their anxiety. These strategies include On The Spot Deep Breathing and Move My Muscles Relaxation.

THINK Strong Thoughts — Building on from being AWARE and keeping CALM, the third step in the ACTION plan teaches children to THINK positively and confidently. Children learn strategies for turning Scared (unhelpful) thoughts into Strong (positive) thoughts.

Get INTO ACTION — The fourth step in the ACTION plan encourages children to gradually deal with anxiety-provoking situations using an ACTION Ladder (a step-by-step graded exposure hierarchy). Children practise the Be AWARE, Keep CALM and THINK Strong Thoughts steps while climbing their ACTION Ladder/s. Children are encouraged to reward themselves for taking ACTION against their anxiety.

Use my OPTIONS — The fifth step in the ACTION plan teaches children additional strategies (or OPTIONS) to further manage their anxiety including problem solving, asking supportive others for help, and positive self-statements. Children are also taught social skills (e.g., confident body signals, assertiveness, dealing with bullying strategies) to further enhance their coping abilities.

NEVER stop taking ACTION — The last step in the ACTION plan encourages children to plan for anxiety-provoking times so they can keep taking ACTION against anxiety in the future.

How the ACTION plan works

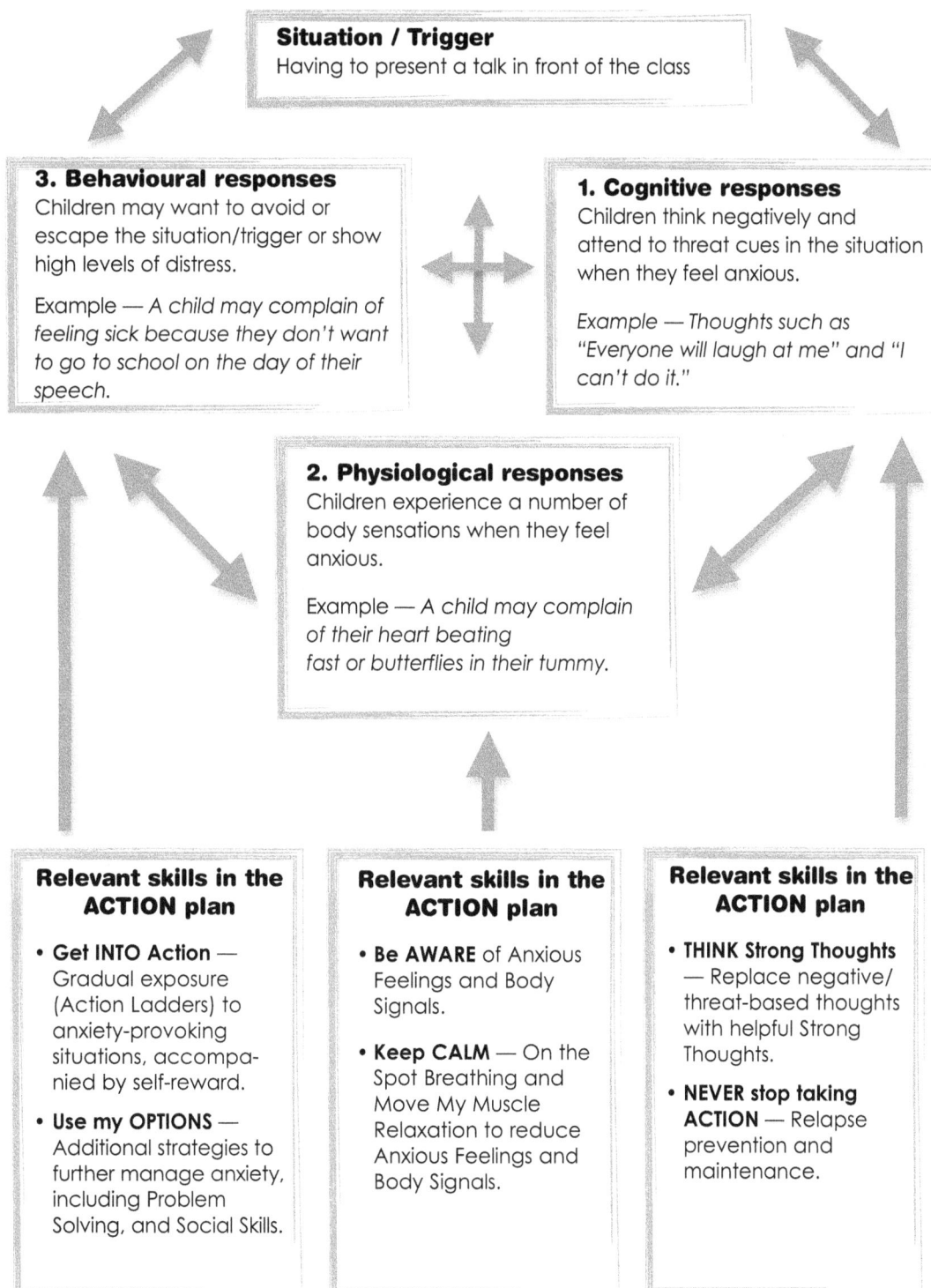

Situation / Trigger
Having to present a talk in front of the class

3. Behavioural responses
Children may want to avoid or escape the situation/trigger or show high levels of distress.

Example — *A child may complain of feeling sick because they don't want to go to school on the day of their speech.*

1. Cognitive responses
Children think negatively and attend to threat cues in the situation when they feel anxious.

Example — *Thoughts such as "Everyone will laugh at me" and "I can't do it."*

2. Physiological responses
Children experience a number of body sensations when they feel anxious.

Example — *A child may complain of their heart beating fast or butterflies in their tummy.*

Relevant skills in the ACTION plan

- **Get INTO Action** — Gradual exposure (Action Ladders) to anxiety-provoking situations, accompanied by self-reward.
- **Use my OPTIONS** — Additional strategies to further manage anxiety, including Problem Solving, and Social Skills.

Relevant skills in the ACTION plan

- **Be AWARE** of Anxious Feelings and Body Signals.
- **Keep CALM** — On the Spot Breathing and Move My Muscle Relaxation to reduce Anxious Feelings and Body Signals.

Relevant skills in the ACTION plan

- **THINK Strong Thoughts** — Replace negative/threat-based thoughts with helpful Strong Thoughts.
- **NEVER stop taking ACTION** — Relapse prevention and maintenance.

Take Action

Personal Goals

In the Take Action program, your child will learn to reduce their anxiety.

Activity

Think about the goals that you have for your child (e.g., I want him/her to be able to sleep in his bed without the light on).

Write your Take ACTION Goals for your child on the lines below:

_____

_____

_____

_____

Think about the goals you have for yourself (e.g., I want to learn how to help my child to keep calm when he/she goes to school).

Write your own Take ACTION Goals on the lines below:

_____

_____

_____

_____

We will review these goals during the program. Share these goals with your child so they know everyone on their Strong Team will be working together.

Be AWARE: Anxiety is a Good Alarm and a False Alarm

As discussed earlier, it was very important for the caveman to feel scared if he saw a sabre-tooth tiger. As soon as the caveman saw the sabre-tooth tiger, the caveman's brain would send messages of danger to his body, making his heart beat fast and his hands cold. These changes in his body would help him to take ACTION and survive because he could either fight the tiger if he had to, or run away from the tiger to safety.

Children and adults get the same changes in their bodies today. If we have to fight or escape from a dangerous situation, our bodies change to help us to be Strong and take ACTION. This is when anxiety is helpful to us! It is normal to feel scared when you are in real danger — just like the caveman.

A certain amount of anxiety in performance situations, such as sporting events, can also be useful (see figure below). However, if anxiety levels become too high it can stop children from doing things properly and they often avoid situations altogether.

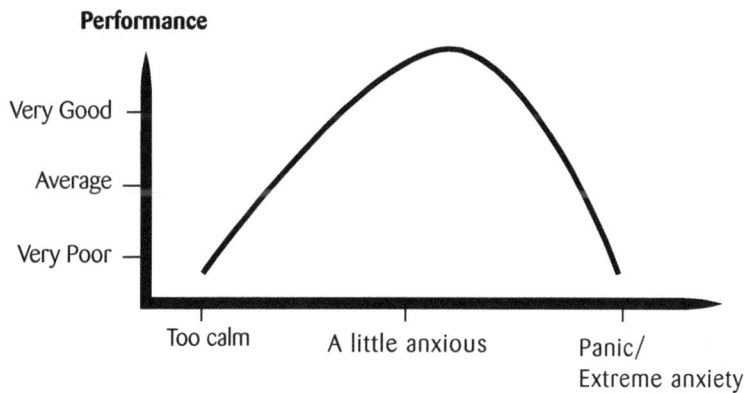

Performance

Very Good —

Average —

Very Poor —

Too calm   A little anxious   Panic/
                                            Extreme anxiety

Sometimes children have 'false alarms' and they feel scared in their bodies when there is no real danger. Children only THINK there is danger. When there is a 'false alarm', children feel Hot on the Feelometer when they should feel Cool (this is happening to the boy below). Help your child to be AWARE of these 'false alarms', by encouraging them to work out how anxious they feel on the Feelometer.

What if my friends don't talk to me tomorrow?

False ALARM

Take Action

Be AWARE of Anxious Feelings

Feelometer

A great way for children to work out how anxious they are feeling in different situations is to use the Feelometer.

Look at the **Feelometer** below:

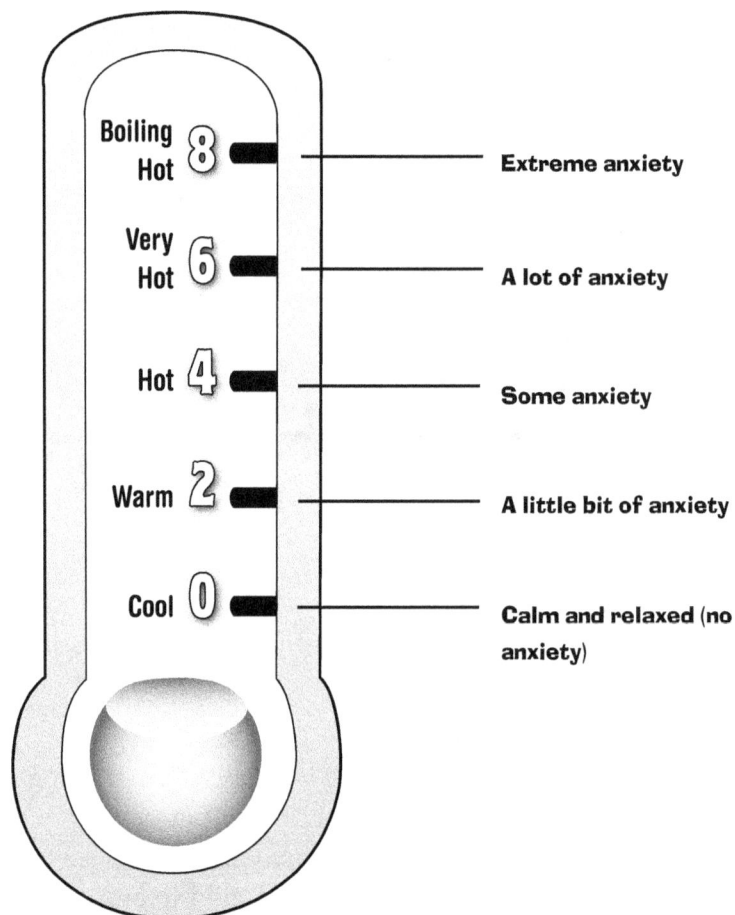

Feelometer	
Boiling Hot **8**	Extreme anxiety
Very Hot **6**	A lot of anxiety
Hot **4**	Some anxiety
Warm **2**	A little bit of anxiety
Cool **0**	Calm and relaxed (no anxiety)

Activity
Feelometer

Your child is learning to use the Feelometer to be aware of their anxious feelings. The Feelometer is also a useful tool for parents to help their child identify anxious feelings in different situations. Think about your child's anxiety levels in relation to ratings on the Feelometer.

Write down a time when your child is CALM and relaxed (Cool on the Feelometer):

_____

_____

Write down a time when your child feels A little bit of anxiety (Warm on the Feelometer):

_____

_____

Write down a time when your child feels Some anxiety (Hot on the Feelometer):

_____

_____

Write down a time when your child feels A lot of anxiety (Very Hot on the Feelometer):

_____

_____

Write down a time when your child feels Extreme anxiety (Boiling Hot on the Feelometer):

_____

_____

ACTION Parents Can Take

As a parent, you can help your child learn to be aware of their anxious feelings by prompting them to rate how they are feeling on the Feelometer. Once AWARE that they are feeling anxious, your child will be able to take ACTION.

Activity
Be AWARE of
Anxious Body Signals

Your child is learning to work out which Anxious Body Signals they get when they feel anxious.

Colour-in the Anxious Body Signals that you have noticed or your child has talked about when they feel anxious. Add in any other Anxious Body Signals that are not listed.

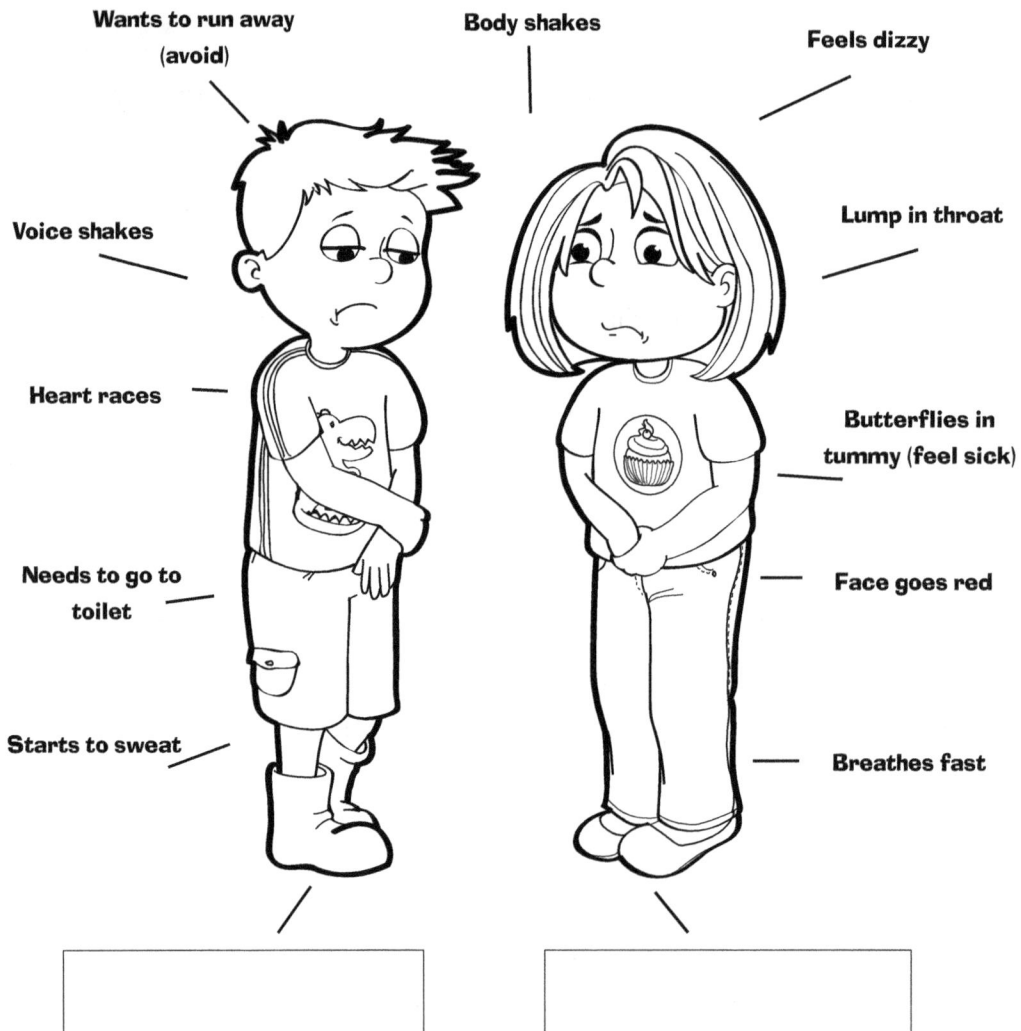

Wants to run away (avoid)

Body shakes

Feels dizzy

Voice shakes

Lump in throat

Heart races

Butterflies in tummy (feel sick)

Needs to go to toilet

Face goes red

Starts to sweat

Breathes fast

Add in any other Anxious Body Signals that are not listed.

ACTION Parents Can Take

Helping your child to be AWARE of their Anxious Body Signals is very important. Once they are AWARE of their Anxious Body Signals, they will be able to keep CALM and relaxed — this is the second step in the ACTION plan!

Activity
Be AWARE of Anxious Feelings

Faces are another way children can be aware of feelings. Look at the faces below and write down the correct feeling. Think about how your child would show each feeling.

What feeling/s is this face showing?

_____

How often does your child feel this way?

_____

What feeling/s is this face showing?

_____

How often does your child feel this way?

_____

What feeling/s is this face showing?

_____

How often does your child feel this way?

_____

What feeling/s is this face showing?

_____

How often does your child feel this way?

_____

ACTION Parents Can Take

As a parent, you can help your child to know how he or she is feeling so they can take ACTION to go from Hot to Cool on the Feelometer and stop 'false alarms'. In anxious situations, encourage your child to **Stop**, **Look** for clues in the environment and people's faces, and **Learn** from their body signals so they can take ACTION.

C Keep CALM

Once children learn to be AWARE of signs of anxiety, the second step in the ACTION plan teaches children strategies to keep CALM.

The first way to keep CALM is to practise On the Spot Deep Breathing.

Deep Breathing can be used whenever children need it and no one has to know they are doing it. That's why it's called "On the Spot" Deep Breathing. It helps children to stay CALM and not let their Anxious Body Signals bother them.

This is how your child is being taught to use Breathing:

1. Place one hand on your stomach and one hand on your chest. Imagine you have a balloon in your stomach and you want to blow it up real big. This means you have to push the air you breathe in all the way down into your stomach.

2. Slowly breathe in through your nose, counting to 3 and "blow up the balloon" in your stomach (make it big like the balloon above). Your chest should not move, only your stomach. Watch to see that only your hand on your stomach goes up as you "fill the balloon with air".

3. Hold your breath while you keep the balloon filled with air and say **Relax** to yourself.

4. Slowly breathe out through your nose counting to 3. The balloon in your stomach will get smaller when you breathe out, and the hand on your stomach should go down.

5. Hold your breath and say **Relax** to yourself.

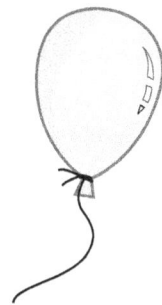

Each time your child practises Deep Breathing they must blow the imaginary balloon UP and DOWN in their stomach at least 5 times.

Activity

Write down times when your child could use Deep Breathing to keep CALM?

_____

How would you know that your child needed to use Deep Breathing to keep CALM?

_____

Write down how you could prompt your child to use Deep Breathing?

_____

The second way to keep CALM is to practise Move My Muscles Relaxation.

Relaxation works really well in getting rid of the tightness in your child's muscles. Relaxing their muscles will make your child feel CALM and not worry about their Anxious Body Signals. In this Relaxation exercise, your child needs to tense and then relax each muscle from their face to their feet.

This is how your child is being taught to use Relaxation:

1. **FACE:** Screw up your face (including your nose and eyes) and count to 3. Pretend that you have just smelt something really bad. Then say **Relax.**

2. **SHOULDERS:** Shrug your shoulders upwards — try to make them touch your ears — and count to 3. Then say **Relax** to yourself and drop your shoulders down again.

3. **HANDS:** Squeeze your fingers together, like you are squeezing a ball and count to 3. Then say **Relax** to yourself and let your fingers relax.

4. **STOMACH:** Pull your stomach in and pretend you are trying to squeeze through a very small gap in a wall. Count to 3. Then say **Relax** to yourself and push your stomach out again.

5. **LEGS:** Make your legs really straight and tighten all the muscles in your legs. Count to 3. Then say **Relax** to yourself and make your legs all floppy (like a rag doll).

6. **FEET:** Clench and point your toes towards the floor. Count to 3. Then say **Relax** to yourself, roll your feet around in circles and unclench your toes.

Activity

Write down times when your child could use Relaxation to keep CALM?

_____

How would you know that your child needed to use Relaxation to keep CALM?

_____

Write down how you could prompt your child to use Relaxation?

_____

Take Action

ACTION Parents Can Take

You have learnt two ways to help your child to keep CALM. Encourage your child to practise their Deep Breathing and Muscle Relaxation whenever they are AWARE of feeling anxious! It is important that parents are AWARE of their child's Anxious Feelings and Body Signals so that children can be prompted to keep CALM.

Ways for your child to feel good

It is important that your child does other 'feel good' activities so that they can learn that there are other positive feelings to experience in life.

Below is a list of things that often make children feel good. Tick the activities that your child could do to feel good. Most of these activities have been chosen as they are relatively low cost to families. Add any other OPTIONS you can THINK of to the end of the list.

Household activities

- ☐ Listening to music
- ☐ Quiet time alone
- ☐ Reading
- ☐ Sleeping
- ☐ Art — drawing, painting, crafts
- ☐ Using Stress ball
- ☐ "Pleasures book" — lists or pictures of things that make your child happy
- ☐ Watching TV shows
- ☐ Playing games — computer games, card games, board games
- ☐ Writing a letter or email to a relative
- ☐ Doing puzzles
- ☐ Talking to a family member, a friend, or a pet — share the problem
- ☐ Help somebody
- ☐ Write things down
- ☐ Doing home plays, playing charades

Social activities

- ☐ Have a sleepover at a friends, or go hang out at their house
- ☐ Rent a movie and make popcorn

Sporting activities

- ☐ Riding a bike
- ☐ Skateboarding or skating
- ☐ Walking or running (taking a pet for a walk)
- ☐ Bouncing on trampoline
- ☐ Throwing a ball around together
- ☐ Playing their favourite sport (e.g. tennis, swimming, basketball)
- ☐ Gardening
- ☐ Dancing

Excursions/community activities

- ☐ Going to the park
- ☐ Fishing
- ☐ Camping
- ☐ Hiking
- ☐ Going to the library
- ☐ Visiting museums or historical buildings
- ☐ Going out for ice-cream or favourite treat
- ☐ Visiting neighbours or relatives
- ☐ Going bowling
- ☐ Collecting rocks/shells/leaves
- ☐ Going to the beach

Take Action

T THINK Strong Thoughts

Building on from being AWARE and keeping CALM, the third step in the ACTION plan teaches children to THINK positively and confidently. Children will learn strategies for turning Scared (unhelpful) thoughts into Strong (positive) thoughts

Activity

Can you recall a time your child OVERESTIMATED THE RISK/DANGER in a situation?

What was the situation?

_____

What happened?

_____

_____

Can you recall a time your child UNDERESTIMATED THEIR ABILITY TO COPE in a situation?

What was the situation?

_____

What happened?

_____

_____

ACTION Parents Can Take

You can help your child to challenge overestimations of risk and danger by prompting them to look for evidence both for and against their scary thoughts; by helping them devise a coping plan for situations in which they feel they cannot cope, and by helping them to learn that their thoughts are not scary. It is also helpful for parents to monitor their own thoughts and take note of the times they might overestimate risk, underestimate their coping and/or be concerned about their own thoughts. In these cases, it is helpful if parents can refrain from sharing their scared thoughts with children and instead, identify strong thoughts that help children to approach difficult situations with realistic expectations and coping plans.

Take ACTION Parenting Strategies: Increasing Strong behaviour

Parents can assist children in managing their anxiety through the following effective and well-researched strategies:

Be on the look out for Strong behaviour in your child

Keep an eye on what your child is doing and look for times when your child is being Strong. What constitutes Strong behaviour may differ between children, but it might include approaching a situation that has scared them in the past or trying a new activity. Paying attention to Strong behaviour will increase the likelihood that your child will repeat the (Strong) behaviour.

Reward Strong behaviour

It is important to reward your child's Strong behaviour — the behaviour that you want repeated. Try to reward the Strong behaviour with praise and / or physical affection immediately after the behaviour occurs. For example, a parent may give their child a hug and say, "You did really well just then — you were able to talk to that new person for 15 minutes". Praise is very powerful and it helps your child identify their strengths and capabilities.

Praise can include acknowledging your child's efforts in a clear and specific way (e.g., "I noticed you tried hard to keep CALM then, that's great!") and / or showing him/her signs of affection (e.g., smile, nod, hug). Give physical affection to your child when they are being Strong, not to soothe their anxiety. Soothing their anxious behaviour instead of Strong behaviour can inadvertently make children engage in the anxious behaviour more often. Be enthusiastic and express your pleasure in your child's efforts, not just their successes.

A reward or a special privilege can also be given to encourage your child to repeat Strong behaviour. The more you reward Strong behaviour, the less likely it is that your child will engage in anxious behaviour as they will be receiving your attention for positive, Strong behaviour.

Model CALM and Strong behaviour

It is important that parents act as CALM and Strong role models for their children, by keeping CALM, voicing Strong Thoughts (and avoid voicing Scared Thoughts) and approaching situations rather than avoiding them. If a child sees a parent keeping CALM and in control, they are more likely to believe they can take ACTION against their anxiety. Parents should encourage children to behave in a CALM and Strong way, just like them.

Parenting anxious children can be challenging at times. When this is the case, it is important that you are AWARE of your own thoughts and feelings, try to keep CALM and interact with your child in a positive way. Just as children have their own Strong Team, it can be beneficial for parents to speak with family and friends when these challenges arise.

Spend 'feel good' and 'talk time' with your child

Spend quality time with your child doing 'feel good' activities, like reading or playing with them. This will help children to learn that happy times can be experienced.

To help your child manage their own anxiety, encourage them to share their experiences and thoughts with you. Spend time talking with your child about their day and how they can use the steps in the ACTION plan to manage their anxiety. Try not to trivialise a child's fears or concerns. This support and understanding will nurture a sense of trust between yourself and your child. Most importantly, encourage and support your child to approach their fears and concerns and deal with them, rather than avoid them. Also, avoid "solving the problem" for your child by taking the ACTION your child might have needed to take. Always evaluate how your child went when they take ACTION against their anxiety and reward Strong behaviour. Spending 'talk time' with your child will ensure they will be more likely to talk to you about future experiences.

Take ACTION Parenting Strategies: Decreasing anxious behaviour

Refocusing anxious behaviour

In the same way that giving your child attention for being Strong will increase this behaviour, giving attention to anxious behaviour (e.g., excessive talking about the situation, delaying or avoiding the situation) will make it more likely that your child will feel anxious in the situation again. Parents can help refocus anxious behaviour by acknowledging their child's anxiety in the situation, and then prompting them to use the steps in the ACTION plan. Parents can help shift the balance from anxious to Strong behaviour by reminding children about "false alarms", encouraging them to use their Keep CALM and Strong THOUGHTS strategies, and to get INTO Action by taking small steps to deal with their fears.

Strong Behaviour

Anxious Behaviour

Make a plan

It is also helpful to make a clear plan with your child about situations that warrant reassurance (i.e., 'real' alarms) versus those that do not (i.e., 'false' alarms). Encourage your child to ask themselves "which one is it" before they come to you for reassurance, and let them know your job is to help them to Take Action. Encourage them to reassure themselves with Strong thoughts. Sometimes, this might mean ignoring reassurance seeking and using praise for Strong behaviour to refocus anxiety.

Avoid excessive reassurance

It is useful for parents to reassure their child that they can act in a Strong way (e.g., keep CALM and THINK Strong thoughts). However, excessive reassurance is less helpful to children because they may then believe they need this reassurance each time the situation occurs. Also, excessive reassurance only relieves anxiety in the short-term and the time taken to provide additional reassurance can delay taking Action. Once you have reassured your child, refocus anxious behaviour by prompting them to use the steps in the Action plan.

Be consistent

It is important that you are consistent with the Take ACTION parenting strategies. It is important to let other family members know about the strategies you will be using to decrease your child's anxious behaviour, so consistency takes place across settings as well.

Get INTO Action

The fourth step in the ACTION plan encourages children to gradually confront anxiety-provoking situations using an ACTION Ladder (a step-by-step exposure hierarchy).

Why is it important for your child to practise and approach scary situations?

Children who are anxious often engage in safety behaviours (e.g., gain excessive reassurance; be highly organised; carry a lucky charm) and avoidance of scary situations.

Consequences of safety behaviours include:

- Children believe that they cannot approach situations without engaging in the safety behaviour. For example, a child who worries a lot about doing well at school might not be able to take a test unless they have studied excessively beforehand. This increases the likelihood that they will engage in the safety behaviour again next time.

- If children do approach the scary situation, they are likely to attribute any success to the safety behaviour. For example, a child who worries a lot about being late for school might always want their parents to take a certain route to school. Being on time is then attributed to taking that route — the safety behaviour — when in reality they were unlikely to run late regardless of the route taken.

Consequences of avoiding scary situations include:

- The fear is strengthened or reinforced. For example, a child who avoids spiders will continue to perceive spiders as scary.

- Children miss out on learning opportunities that might disprove or disconfirm their Scared Thoughts and provide evidence to support Strong Thoughts. For example, a child who avoids reading in front of the class will not learn that they can cope with this situation and do a good job!

- Children miss the opportunity to practise developmentally appropriate skills. For example, a child who avoids speaking with peers will not gain practice in conversation skills. Children need to be reminded that people develop confidence by frequently practising their skills (e.g., elite sportspeople) and learning from their mistakes.

ACTION Parents Can Take

Parents can assist their child by validating their fears (e.g., "I can see you are feeling scared at the moment...") but avoiding excessive verbal reassurance. This can inadvertently enable your child to delay dealing with the feared situation. Try to acknowledge your child's fears and encourage them to take ACTION (without their safety behaviours). You can help remind your child about the importance of approaching situations, instead of avoiding them.

There are several key features to creating a successful ACTION Ladder

1. One step at a time

The first step in the ACTION Ladder must be something that your child can do already. It is better to err on the side of choosing a situation which is easier than expected, rather than choosing something daunting and your child feeling unable to proceed, or feeling overwhelmed. Fears can be made worse if a child suddenly forces himself or herself, without sufficient preparation, to confront something that has been avoided or which is perceived as extremely threatening. The steps on the ACTION Ladder should not be too far apart and must be achievable during the Take Action program.

2. Stay until CALM

It is very important that your child remains in the situation until their anxiety begins to decrease. Children should feel Cool on the Feelometer before leaving the situation. Children may get worried about this and THINK "How bad could the anxiety get?" Remember anxiety only increases to a certain level and then declines, even when children do not use calming strategies to help this process. Children must stay in the scary situation until they feel CALM so they learn that they can cope and the situation is not that scary — they just THINK it is! Your child needs to practise the skills in the ACTION plan, especially Keep CALM and using Strong Thoughts, while climbing their ACTION Ladder.

3. Practise often — First time, Second time, Third time

Just confronting a situation once will not be enough to take away your child's anxiety completely. It takes many repetitions, as well as using the skills in the ACTION Plan, to "wear down" the anxiety associated with a given situation. This frequent practise will result in your child feeling less and less anxious in the same situation. The more frequently a situation is confronted the sooner the degree of anxiety will begin to reduce. Remember that approaching and practising the skills in the ACTION Plan when in scary situations decreases anxiety.

4. Practise in lots of situations and with lots of different stimuli that trigger anxiety.

For example, if your child is afraid of vomiting, they could practise eating food from the food court in a local shopping centre; at a birthday party; and the deli. They could do high impact exercise that increases physical arousal. Your child could also practise with a variety of feared foods, such as crunchy and lumpy textures, reheated food, and any food items they specifically avoid. The key message is that practising the ACTION Plan in lots of situations and with lots of stimuli that triggers fear is likely to strengthen anxiety reductions.

Take Action

Obstacles in creating an ACTION Ladder

ACTION Ladders are one of the most important strategies learnt in the Take ACTION Program. It is important to THINK about what obstacles may hinder your child's progress in climbing their ACTION Ladder. Tick which of the following obstacles below may be relevant for you and your child.

Activity

☐ Safety behaviours e.g., excessive reassurance (please describe)

_____

☐ Avoidance (please describe)

_____

☐ Communicating your own fears to your child (please describe)

_____

☐ Your child not completing the entire step on the ACTION Ladder (please describe)

_____

☐ Your child not practising often enough (please describe)

_____

☐ Your child not staying in the situation until CALM (please describe)

_____

☐ Appropriate rewards (please describe)

_____

☐ Worries that this might cause the distress in your child (please describe)

_____

ACTION Parents Can Take

Be AWARE of these obstacles over the coming weeks and use the Take ACTION strategies to overcome the obstacles. Remember the more your child takes ACTION, the faster their anxiety will decrease.

ⓞ Use my OPTIONS

The fifth step in the ACTION plan teaches children additional strategies (or OPTIONS) to further manage their anxiety.

Activity

The first OPTION is Problem Solving

Children learn to solve problems by thinking about the best ACTION to take. They record a Scared thought in the Option One bubble and what ACTION he/she would take. Then they write a Strong Thought in Option 2 and what ACTION he/she would take. They learn to solve problems by weighing up their ACTIONS. Encourage your child to follow these steps when they have a problem. Write the situation in the box below and follow the Problem Solving steps.

1. Thought OPTIONS
List two of the thoughts your child could have about this scary time.

2. What type of thought is this (scared; strong)?

3. What ACTION would your child take if he/she thought this way?

Option One

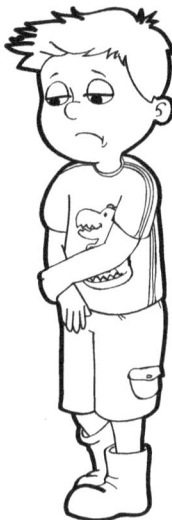

Option Two

4. Weigh up the OPTIONS — What is the best Option for your child to choose (Look at the ACTION column to decide)?_____

5. Take ACTION — Your child needs to act out the best Option. (Look at the Action column to decide).

> The following 11 handouts are taken from the Take Action Child Workbook so that parents understand what children are working on during the Use my OPTIONS and NEVER stop taking ACTION modules.

Take Action

The second OPTION is a Strong Team

A Strong Team is a list of people who can help you to feel Strong and take ACTION against your anxiety. Strong Team members are positive people who can remind you of the steps in the ACTION plan.

Activity
Think of people that could be on your Strong Team.

Choose people from home (e.g., parents), school (e.g., teacher) and other areas of your life (e.g., sporting coach) so you can always have a Strong Team member close by. Write your Strong Team members on the lines below.

My Strong Team members are:

1._____

2._____

3._____

4._____

5._____

What situations could your Strong Team members help you with?

_____

_____

What could your Strong Team members do to help you (e.g., listen to you, remind you of the skills in the ACTION plan)?

_____

_____

Ask the people you listed above if they will be part of your Strong Team. Tell your Strong Team members what situations they can help you with, and how they can best help you to take ACTION against anxiety.

The third OPTION is to Focus on the Positives

Remember from the THINK Strong Thoughts module that Strength Sayings are catchy sayings that will help you to feel Strong as you are taking ACTION against anxiety.

Some examples of Strength Sayings are:

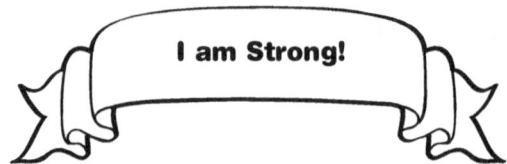

I can do it!

I am Strong!

Activity

Now that you have more experience Being Strong by doing your ACTION Ladder, think about some more Strength Sayings that you can use to keep feeling Strong.

Write your Strength Sayings in the ribbons below:

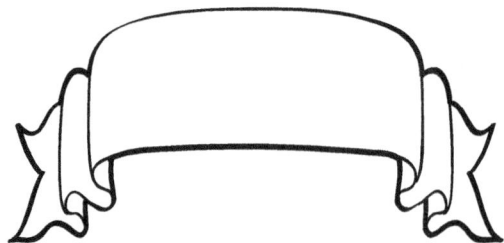

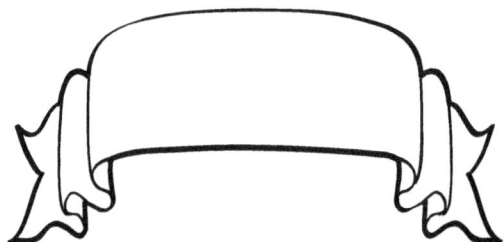

Take Action

Keep Being Positive

Here are helpful things you can do to keep Being Positive:

**Keep your body active
and try new things!**

Smile a lot!

**Think about nice
things you enjoy!**

**Believe in yourself
and never give up!**

Doing these things
helps you to be Strong
like Dulcy and Dion
the dolphins.

The fourth OPTION is having Confident Body Signals

Children who get anxious often find it hard to talk to other people and stand up for themselves, and they might get bullied. Showing Confident Body Signals can help you to be confident, assertive and deal with bullies.

Remember back to when you learnt about Anxious Body Signals (e.g. fast beating heart). You now know how to keep CALM (by using On the Spot Deep Breathing and Move my Muscles Relaxation) to reduce these Anxious Body Signals.

Confident Body Signals help you to look Confident in social situations (e.g. talking with a friend at school). There is an easy way to remember your Confident Body Signals — just remember to:

SMILE

S SMILE and face the other person!

M MAKE eye contact and look interested while you are talking with the other person.

I INITIATE the conversation.
Remember to:
- Use a greeting (e.g., "Hello") when introducing yourself
- Pick a topic that you both like to talk about
- Ask questions

L LISTEN to the other person.

E ENJOY yourself and relax:
- Use On the Spot Deep Breathing
- Remember your Strength Sayings
- Keep smiling

The fifth OPTION is Being Confident and Assertive

Look at the three different ways that you can act towards other children and adults below.

The Shy Starfish Way

Whatever you say, I'll do

Acting like the Shy Starfish means you might ignore the situation or 'give in' to the other person. You do not say how you feel about the situation.

- **Feelings:** Shy, embarrassed, nervous, unhappy.

- **Body Signals:** Talk softly like a mouse, mumble, look down at the floor, stand far away, hunch over, feel Hot on the Feelometer.

- **You might say things like:** "Whatever you say", "I don't know", "If you say so".

- **Actions:** You might do things like walk away, not be able to say NO, give the other person what they want (even if you don't want to!), avoid the problem, get upset.

Do you think that this is a good way to act?

☐ YES ☐ NO

The Angry Shark Way

You better do this for me or else...

Acting like the Angry Shark means you attack the other person, over-react, or get angry at the other person.

- **Feelings:** Angry, annoyed, out of control, mean.

- **Body signals:** Stand close to the other person, look angry, have tight muscles and clenched fists, feel Hot on the Feelometer.

- **You might say things like:** "You'd better do this for me", "If you don't do this, watch out", "I want this now".

- **Actions:** You might do things like look angry, threaten, push, hit, kick, shout yell, speak rudely or tease.

Do you think that this is a good way to act?

☐ YES   ☐ NO

Take Action

The Strong Dolphin Way: Being Confident and Assertive

I would like to do it this way

Acting like the Strong Dolphin means you say how you feel and speak up for yourself in an honest, polite and friendly way. This is called being Assertive!

- **Feelings:** Happy, confident, in control and you feel good about yourself.

- **Body signals:** Stand tall, smile, look CALM, look others in the eyes, feel Cool on the Feelometer.

- **You might say things like:** "I THINK that…", "Let's try", "I would like to do it this way".

- **Actions:** You might do things like speak firmly but friendly, be confident and relaxed, listen to the other person's point of view, speak up for your rights, find a solution to the problem and make more friends.

Do you think that this is a good way to act?

☐ **YES** ☐ **NO**

Acting like the Strong Dolphin means you are being Confident and Assertive. This is the best way to act towards other people!

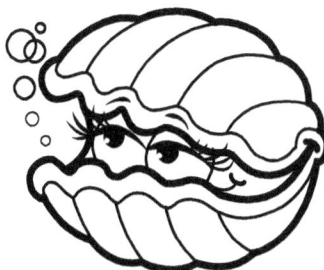

3 Steps to being Confident and Assertive

Dulcy would like to act in a Confident and Assertive way with her friend but she doesn't know how to. Dulcy's friend borrowed her swimming cap three weeks ago and she hasn't given it back to her. Dulcy really needs her swimming cap so she can keep climbing her ACTION Ladder of swimming to school by herself. Let's help Dulcy to be Confident and Assertive by following the steps below.

Step One: Tell the other person what you think the problem is

> Sally, when you borrowed my swimming cap three weeks ago, I thought you would give it back to me after your lesson.

Step Two: Tell the other person how you feel about the problem

> I feel annoyed that you haven't given my swimming cap back.

Step Three: Tell the other person a solution to the problem

> I would really like it if you gave me my swimming cap back today.

Things to remember when being Confident and Assertive:
- Use your Confident Body Signals (SMILE).
- Keep CALM by doing On the Spot Deep Breathing.
- THINK Strong Thoughts.
- Discuss the solution you have thought of with the other person. Remember to listen to their point of view as well!

Congratulate yourself if you tried to be Confident and Assertive!!

Take Action

Steps for Dealing with Bullying

Step One: Stop what you are doing and practise your On the Spot Deep Breathing. This will help you to keep CALM.

Step Two: THINK about the OPTIONS that you have in the situation. Some Strong and Confident OPTIONS to choose from are:

Walk away

Tell an adult

Ignore the bullying if you can

Say "I heard what you said and I don't really care"

Tell them firmly and calmly to leave you alone

Imagine there is a force field all around you protecting you from their words

Step Three: Decide on the best Option and take ACTION. Say how you feel in a Confident and Assertive way (like the Strong Dolphin).

Things to remember when Dealing with Bullying:

• Use your Confident Body Signals (SMILE).

• Keep CALM by doing On the Spot Deep Breathing.

• THINK Strong Thoughts.

• Do not yell or scream, call them names, or be physically aggressive.

Congratulate yourself if the Option you chose worked!

Take Action

N Step Six

I will NEVER stop taking ACTION against anxiety

You have done a great job learning to Take ACTION against anxiety

You have learnt six steps in the ACTION plan to help you deal with anxiety. It is important that you NEVER stop taking ACTION in the future.

By planning for times in the future when you may need your ACTION plan, you will already be prepared and Strong!

Activity

For each of the six steps in the ACTION plan, write down the skills that will help you take ACTION against anxiety in the future.

A Be AWARE

_____

C Keep CALM

_____

T THINK Strong Thoughts

_____

I Get INTO Action

_____

O Use my OPTIONS

_____

N NEVER stop taking ACTION

_____

Take Action

Home Task
Parent Monitoring Diary

Use the Parent Monitoring Diary below to help understand your child's anxiety better.

Date & Time	Describe the anxious situation	Rating of child's anxiety on Feelometer	What showed you that your child was anxious (e.g. Body Signals)?	What did your child do (e.g., avoid) or say?	What did you do or say?

www.ingramcontent.com/pod-product-compliance
Lightning Source LLC
Chambersburg PA
CBHW080847270326
41934CB00013B/3231